This n… belongs to: